PM Non-fictio
Maths Around Us
TEACHERS' GUIDE

Red Level

ELSIE NELLEY

NELSON PRICE MILBURN

Contents

About the PM Library   3

Using this Teachers' Guide   5

The non-fiction books at Red Level   7

    Tall Things   8

    Eggs for Breakfast   10

    Red and Blue and Yellow   12

    Look Up, Look Down   14

    Two Eyes, Two Ears   16

    A Roof and a Door   18

Using the Blackline masters   20

Blackline masters 1–12   21

About the PM Library

Non-fiction books

The basic philosophy

'Children learn best with books that have meaning and are rewarding'... *Reading in Junior Classes*, New Zealand Department of Education.

'I can read this!' All books in the PM Library are **centred on meaning**, and are also designed to give children the rewarding experience of **success**. If a child can read one book they should be able to read another and another. Success should follow success. When the right match of 'child to book' is made, the greater the child's interest and the greater his or her desire to read.

On every page in every book care is taken with the sentence structures, the choice of words, the clear well-spaced type, and with the meaningful, accurate illustrations. Because the books are easy as well as interesting, children are able to practise a variety of reading skills and enjoy the feedback of success. They learn new words — and practise them again and again — all the time understanding what they are reading about, and returning to the books with pleasure *because* they have real meaning, and emotional impact.

The authors of the PM Library have worked hard to combine the virtues of two approaches — **controlled basic vocabulary** to let children master a growing number of common but confusing **high frequency** words, and **storytelling** quality to engage the mind and emotions and make learning to read satisfying. The authors have been well supported by a team of highly talented illustrators and photographers.

The PM Library Non-fiction strand

There are six non-fiction titles at each colour level of the PM Library. The fiction and non-fiction titles are closely linked in content, as well as in the use of vocabulary and language structures. Each non-fiction title has been carefully written using the same vocabulary and new-word ratios as the story books at the same colour level, letting children experience success.

Many children prefer reading non-fiction to stories. Factual texts fascinate and inform them about the world around them and the things in it in which they are most interested. Well thought through factual texts are entirely relevant and interpretable to the child. Truth, reliability and accuracy are qualities the whole

community values. Truth and respect for the real world in all its diversity are very much part of the PM meaning-driven philosophy, and this is evident in the PM Non-fiction titles.

All PM books are shaped by a concern for logic and accuracy. Newspaper reporters and photographers know that truth is a reality — children, too, enjoy non-fiction for the same reasons. Many children respond to the measurement concepts in *Tall Things*, the emotions underlying *My Dad*, the technology (and emotions!) of *The Dentist*, the beauty and information of *Walking in the Summer*, and the interesting accurate facts packed into *Pets*, *Animals in the Wild* and *Farm Animals*.

Features of the Red, Yellow, Blue and Green Non-fiction books

These include:
- *grading*. The high frequency words in the PM Non-fiction books are closely matched to the high frequency words in the PM Story books. The grading logo on the back covers indicates the recommended level for guided reading: two petals are fully coloured, for example the 'Maths Around Us' books show both a Red 3 petal and a Yellow 1 petal. This shows that the non-fiction books can be slotted in between the colour levels and are bridging books.
- *text construction*. Non-fiction texts have a different construction to that of story books. The necessary introduction of new interest words (mostly nouns) is accompanied by exact picture clues, for example the word 'stethoscope' may already be in the child's oral vocabulary but it could not possibly be decoded by an emergent reader without the support of the photographic clue. Children must learn, when reading non-fiction, to 'read' the text and picture together, as both provide the information.
- *reliable information*. Thorough research and scientific accuracy shape all books in the PM Library, not least the non-fiction books.
- *making connections*. Books have special meaning for small children when they match their own experiences. The topics in the 'Around Us' series of non-fiction are about the world of the very young child: comparing heights, staying with grandparents, visiting the doctor, finding autumn leaves.
- *a cross-curricula resource*. Making connections through language to maths, social studies, health and environmental studies allows children to confirm

what they already know. Making these connections also helps them to consider new ideas.

- *links with other PM Books*. Links between the non-fiction titles and the story books increase the children's understanding and add depth to all strands. Many of the PM Starters and Story Books support the PM Non-fiction books:

  Red Level — *Look Up, Look Down* → *Ben's treasure hunt*
  Yellow Level — *Our Baby* → *The new baby*
  Blue Level — *Our Teacher* → *Come on, Tim*
  Green Level — *Walking in the Winter* → *Father Bear's surprise, Snow on the hill*

The books at Red Level
Maths Around Us

These early non-fiction books emphasise the link between mathematics and language. Through reading the text and looking at the photographs, children will come to understand some early mathematical concepts and be able to apply them to problems arising in every-day life:

Measurement and estimation *Tall Things*
One-to-one correspondence *Eggs for Breakfast*
Recognising and comparing colours *Red and Blue and Yellow*
Space and location *Look Up, Look Down*
Numbers and numeration *Two Ears, Two Eyes*
Shapes *A Roof and a Door*

Each book has been designed to foster a sense of personal achievement as young children discover, interpret and learn about mathematics in the world around them.

The books at Yellow Level
Families Around Us

These books illustrate the fact that families are different; for example, not all children have brothers and sisters, and not all children live with two parents. The emphasis in these books is on family members and how they support and care for one another. The families shown in the books differ, but many of the situations depicted will be familiar and should stimulate children to talk and write about their own experiences.

The books at Blue Level
People Around Us

These books are about the work of responsible caregivers, the people whom most children meet. Some small children are fearful of the doctor, the dentist, or even the hairdresser, and it is helpful if visits to such people are discussed. Although individual experiences may differ, most children will identify with the characters and experiences portrayed in these books. Some children may gain confidence as their knowledge is broadened through discussion. In each book, a child is accompanied by an adult, and procedures are clarified in simple terms. It is useful, for example, if a child knows something about eye tests before a visit to an optometrist.

The books at Green Level
Time and Seasons

Young learners develop concepts about time slowly, as their personal experience grows. These books help children to focus on the small daily or greater seasonal changes that mark the passage of time. Children will be stimulated to discuss, record and illustrate the changes they observe. Common sense demands that children enjoy each 'season' book at the appropriate time of the year, so these four books may sometimes be *read to* children, and sometimes *shared with* them before they can read them *independently*.

Using this Teachers' Guide

Before beginning the PM Non-fiction books at Red Level, children need many opportunities in the company of an adult to increase their spoken vocabulary and book experiences. At this emergent reading level, the child will also practise reading using alphabet books *(PM Alphabet Starters)* and simple structured pre-reading books (PM Starters One and Two). These books will help the child establish the right ideas about directionality and one-to-one matching of spoken and written words. Many of the high frequency basic words that children will use in their own writing occur in these books. When a child is sure of 30–35 basic words (*I, am, is, to, the, a,* etc.) then they will be ready to enjoy the PM Non-fiction books.

This Teachers' Guide has been designed to assist busy teachers to plan and develop challenging language opportunities in their classrooms. The PM Non-fiction books should be used with a wide variety of other books and materials to ensure that children succeed at each level before they proceed to the next. The ideas described in this Teachers' Guide can be adapted for other books.

There are Teachers' Guides for each colour level in the PM Library.

Red   (Daisy clock levels 1, 2, 3)

Yellow (Daisy clock levels 4, 5, 6)

Blue   (Daisy clock levels 7, 8, 9)

Green   (Daisy clock levels 10, 11, 12)

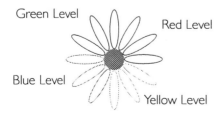

The large daisy logo has eight coloured petals showing the more advanced levels that follow the familiar 12 of the daisy 'clock'. The eight are: Orange (1 and 2), Turquoise (3 and 4), Purple (5 and 6) and Gold (7 and 8).

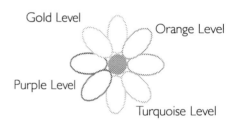

The PM Non-fiction books are intended to be read at the end of a level when children are ready to move onto the next level. The 'People Around Us' books and 'Time and Seasons' books may also be used at Orange and Turquoise levels because, although these books belong to a lower reading level, their subject matter is relevant.

Each Teachers' Guide has suggestions and ideas for guidance in the use of the PM Non-fiction books at that level. Emphasis has been placed upon the development of the language skills — speaking, listening, reading, writing, viewing and presenting. These skills are common to all curriculum areas. Reading is not treated as a subject that stands alone.

1 Teacher information

This section contains a brief summary of the content. It may include background information for the teacher.

2 Curriculum

The PM Non-fiction books are resources which will enhance curriculum delivery. Examples of relevant objectives in language, mathematics, science, social studies or health and physical well-being are included.

3 Creating the atmosphere

This is the 'tuning in' stage. It is the time when the teacher focuses the children's thinking on the content or concepts of the book. Related language or new vocabulary can be discussed, or written on a chart or whiteboard. In this way new ideas become familiar and the children's language is enriched.

4 Focusing on the book
Guided reading

This stage may take place straight after the 'tuning in' stage, or may be delayed until later in the same day or even the next day. Book study is an in-depth study of the book. Teachers will guide children as they read these books, linking existing knowledge with new information and supporting children as required. During this guided reading children will use and develop appropriate reading strategies in a meaningful context. It should be such an enjoyable experience that children will want to read the book right through to the end all by themselves. Because new high frequency words have been introduced slowly and carefully in the books, children can achieve this success.

5 Going beyond the book

Teachers may select from or adapt these language enrichment activities to suit the needs of their own classes. Some activities are suitable for groups of 5–6 children to work on together, others are for individuals. Some may even be taken with a whole class. All have been designed to develop language skills. The activities give children ample opportunity to interact verbally, not only with teachers, but also with one another. Some activities in science and mathematics have been included to extend children's thinking beyond the book content. The language and art activities will allow children opportunities to express themselves and help them to make sense of their reading.

6 Books to share and compare

These are suggested titles by other authors and from other publishers. Children need to have many stories read to them, often. They soon know that reading is enjoyable and will want to return to favourite books to read themselves. Occasional questions about the stories will sharpen the focus, prompt interest and talk and ensure that children listen with understanding.

7 Blackline masters

Blackline masters designed to challenge children's thinking are included with the Non-fiction Teachers' Guides at Red, Yellow, Blue and Green levels. Each activity is for the individual child and can be completed independently and with a sense of success.

From very early stages the children are encouraged to use the PM Non-fiction: Maths Around Us:

- as reference material, e.g. *Red and Blue and Yellow, A Roof and a Door*;
- to follow instructions, e.g. *Eggs for Breakfast, Look Up, Look Down*;
- to record information based on their own experiences, e.g. *Tall Things, Red and Blue and Yellow*;
- to complete a simple checklist, e.g. *Two Eyes, Two Ears, A Roof and a Door*.

The non-fiction books at **Red Level**

Title	Level	Page
Tall Things	3/4	8
Eggs for Breakfast	3/4	10
Red and Blue and Yellow	3/4	12
Look Up, Look Down	3/4	14
Two Eyes, Two Ears	3/4	16
A Roof and a Door	3/4	18

Curriculum

Mathematics — Measurement

The children will:

- show or describe the difference between two heights
- demonstrate an understanding of the words and phrases 'tall', 'tall like' and 'not tall like'

Blackline masters 1 and 2, pp.21–22.

Tall Things

Children's early experiences of height comparison usually involve comparing themselves with objects. *Tall Things* gradually introduces other experiences, including 'tall like' and 'not tall like', as children compare objects of varying heights.

Creating the atmosphere

- Take the children outside to look for things that are tall, e.g. a flagpole, tall trees, or a tall fence around the playground. Ask the children to stand by something that is taller than them.
- Back in the classroom, talk about the things that were taller than the children.

Focusing on the book — guided reading

- Read the title and discuss the cover and title page photographs. Talk about the shape of the book. Talk about the giraffes' long legs and necks.
- pp.2–3 — Point out that each person is looking up at the tall elephant. Encourage the children to talk about their own experiences of looking up at tall things.
- pp.4–5 — Look at the trees that are tall like the giraffes. Ask the children what other things can be tall.
- pp.6–7 — Identify the tall crane and the building. Point out the way the crane appears to go up to the sky. Have the children demonstrate how they would tilt their heads to look up at a crane. Remind the children that they should avoid situations where they would look up at the sun.
- pp.8–9 — Discuss the fact that real skyscrapers are tall, but in this photograph the skyscraper is tall like the girl. Point out what the girl is doing with her hand and encourage the children to talk about other situations when they measure in this way.
- pp.10–11 — Compare the height of the teddy bear with the height of the girl. Discuss how the concept of 'tall' is a comparison between two objects.
- pp.12–15 — Have the children demonstrate where they come up to when measuring themselves with the teacher.
- pp.16 — Discuss the fact that the children are still growing. Look at the photograph and discuss the concept of seriation. Ask the children to find who is the tallest, who is the smallest, who is taller than the teddy bear, etc.

Going beyond the book

- Make a large shared book about tall things. The children can write their own captions using the word tall.

- Ask the children to draw the people in their family in order of size. Ask them to write stories about their families focusing on size comparisons, e.g. 'I am not tall like my dad. My little brother is not tall like me.'

- Ask the children to find a partner. Pin a piece of blank paper on the wall. Ensure that the children keep their heels on the floor as they measure each other to find out their relative heights. Then have the children measure themselves again by standing back-to-back. They can draw themselves with their partners and write captions using the word 'taller'.

- Read pp.10–11 of *Tall Things* again. List things which are not tall like the children. They can write and draw about these things.

- Ask one child to build a tower using ten blocks of different sizes. Make the tower near a wall but not against it. Mark the height that the tower reaches. Ask another child to make the tower taller. Compare the two heights. Talk about the fact that "The tower was this tall, but now it is taller. Now it is this tall."

- Read *Happy Birthday, Sam* (Pat Hutchins, Penguin Books, 1981). Have the children talk about what they can do now that they are tall.

- Bring some soft toys to school. First, put two toys beside each other and discuss with the children which toy is taller. Then compare three toys to find which is the tallest.

- Have the children talk about how tall they might be one day.

Books to share and compare

- **Happy Birthday, Sam**,
  Pat Hutchins,
  Penguin Books, 1981.
- **Jolly Tall**,
  Jane Hissey,
  Red Fox, 1992.
- **Let's Look at Growing**,
  Nicola Tuxworth,
  Lorenz, 1996.
- **Opposites**,
  Nicola Tuxworth,
  Lorenz, 1996.

Curriculum

**Mathematics —
Number comparisons
and relationships**

The children will:
• match related objects in one-to-
  one correspondence
• count to find the number property
  in sets containing up to four
  objects

Eggs for Breakfast

In *Eggs for Breakfast*, one-to-one correspondence and aspects of numeration arise as a table is set for breakfast. As the number 'four' is focused on in the book, children can study this number.

Creating the atmosphere

• Prepare a simple one-to-one correspondence activity. Ask each child in the group to find a pencil and a piece of paper. Seat the children in a circle. Ask them to hold up their pencils and, in turn, say, "I have a pencil." The teacher may reinforce the one-to-one concept by saying "Good. Emma has a pencil."

Focusing on the book — guided reading

• Read the title. Identify the characters in the book from the cover photograph and talk about the sets of four, e.g. four people, four chairs, four mats, etc. Ask the children how many chairs, mats, etc. they would need for their own families at breakfast time.
• Read the title again on the title page and count the eggs to reinforce the number 'four'.
• pp.2–3 — Count the egg cups and the plates. Talk about what each person is doing to help. Discuss which tasks children can do safely, and which ones adults should do.
• pp.4–5 — Discuss the way the mats have been arranged on the table — one on each side of the table. Count the mats.
• pp.6–7 — Count the plates. Discuss the relationship of one plate to one mat.
• pp.8–9 — Count the spoons. Turn back to p.7 and discuss how a spoon will go beside each plate.
• pp.10–11 — Count the eggs on p.10. Count the eggs on the bench and the one on the spoon. Ask the children how many more egg cups will be needed. Talk about how one and three more make four. Notice the glasses of juice that Dad is preparing.
• p.12 — Count the egg cups. Turn back to p.10 and count the eggs. Discuss the concept of one egg for one egg cup.
• p.13 — Study the photograph. Count the four egg cups. Some children may be able to say how many eggs are left in the saucepan.
• pp.14–15 — Discuss again the concept of one egg for one egg cup.
• p.16 — Talk about the table setting — the mats, the plates, the egg cups, the spoons, the glasses of juice. Also talk about the fact that there are four chairs and four people.

**Blackline masters 3 and 4,
pp.23–24.**

Going beyond the book

• Bring some commonly used objects to school. Ask the children to match the related objects together, e.g:

    a toothbrush and a tube of toothpaste

    a brush and a comb

    a saucepan and a lid

    a key and a lock

Eggs for Breakfast

- Bring some table mats, plastic plates, spoons and egg cups to school. Teach the children the following song. Sing it to the tune of 'Here we go round the mulberry bush' (PM Readalongs: On with the Dance).

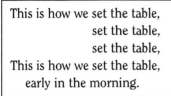 

> This is how we set the table,
> set the table,
> set the table,
> This is how we set the table,
> early in the morning.

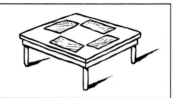

> This is where the mats will go,
> mats will go,
> mats will go,
> This is where the mats will go,
> early in the morning.

Make up other verses using the words *plates*, *cups* and *spoons*. As the children sing the song, one child can 'set the table' for her or his own family by putting the appropriate number of mats, plates, etc. on the table. Another child can count to check that the numbers are correct.

- Have the children make and decorate a mat or a bookmark for each member of their families. Encourage the children to say, "This one is for Mum. This one is for my brother. This one is for me."

- Read *Goldilocks and the Three Bears* (PM Traditional Tales and Plays Turquoise Level). Dramatise the story. Give the children play dough to make bowls for each bear. Ask them to write captions, e.g. 'This bowl is for Father Bear.'

- Collect a variety of plastic jars or bottles with screw tops. Spread out the bottles and the tops on a flat surface. Ask the children to match the tops and bottles together correctly. This activity reinforces one-to-one matching.

- Explore the constancy of the number of elements in sets of up to four elements. Using both words and numerals, the children could:

  make sets of up to four objects to match numeral cards

  put a label card beside a set of up to four objects

  put sets of up to four objects in counting order

  make patterns using up to four objects

  show the similarity between sets by
  matching objects in one-to-one correspondence

Books to share and compare

- **Look and Learn Matching,**
  George Siede and Donna Preis,
  Evans Brothers, 1994.
- **Six Speckled Hens,**
  Babs Bell Hajdusiewicz,
  Shortland, 1997.
- **Take Off with Sorting,**
  Sally Hewitt,
  Evans Brothers, 1995.

Curriculum

Mathematics — Number

The children will:

• classify by colour
• develop vocabulary related to colour

Red and Blue and Yellow

The primary colours red, blue and yellow are dominant in the environment. Children will observe and develop an awareness of these primary colours within their immediate surroundings when they read *Red and Blue and Yellow*.

Creating the atmosphere

• Re-read *Ben's red car* (PM Starters One). Ask a child to find something in the classroom that is red like Ben's car. Ask another child to find something blue, and another child to find something yellow. Talk about things that are often red or blue or yellow.
• Write down some of the children's statements on a large chart.

Focusing on the book — guided reading

• Read the title. Ask the children to name the things that are red, blue and yellow in the cover and title page photographs.
• pp.2–3 — Discuss what the car will do when the lights go red. Talk about how red can signal danger and that it is often used on various stop signs. Ask the children to find other things in the photograph which are also red.
• pp.4–5 — Talk about the boy's red bike, his red shirt and the red stripes on his helmet. Discuss how the boy will have to be careful when riding his bike.
• pp.6–7 — Talk about the blue flower, the blue sky, the boy's blue jumper and the mother's blue shirt. Discuss how blue is a colour often seen in the natural environment, e.g. the sea can be blue.
• pp.8–9 — Point out that while this bird (a budgie) is blue, some budgies can be yellow and others are green.
• pp.10–11 — Ensure the children know that many young chicks are yellow when first born. Talk about the soft fluffy chicks, the yellow corn, the straw and the boy's yellow jumper.
• pp.12–13 — Point out to the children that the teddy bear is soft, fluffy and yellow like the chicks.
• pp.14–15 — Talk about the colours on the school bag — the blue bag, the red pocket, and the yellow zip and straps.
• p.16 — Discuss the colours on the play equipment. Talk about other things around the children that are red, blue and yellow, e.g. 'For Sale' signs, road signs, painted vehicles, etc.

Going beyond the book

• Make a book about the colours red, blue and yellow using *Red and Blue and Yellow* as a model. Write the children's suggestions on the left hand page, and paste the children's paintings and captions on the facing page.

Blackline masters 5 and 6, pp.25–26.

Red and Blue and Yellow

- Make books about each of the colours red, blue and yellow. The children could draw or paint pictures; make red, blue, or yellow finger paintings; glue real objects in, e.g. a red leaf; or make collage pictures using different fabrics in shades of red, blue or yellow.

- Take the children for a walk to identify red, blue and yellow things around the school. The children may be able to collect some things, e.g. yellow buttercups or red autumn leaves. Make a mural about this experience. Write captions using red, blue and yellow marker pens to match the colours of the objects on the mural.

- To extend the previous activity, make relationship charts about red, blue and yellow (see the illustration below). The colour books *Red*, *Blue* and *Yellow* (Gabrielle Woolfitt, Wayland, 1991) will stimulate discussion and help the children to make choices.

- Read *The bumper cars* (PM Story Books Red Level) to the children. In this book, the bumper cars are red and blue. After reading the book, the children could draw the bumper cars, or complete the Blackline master from *New PM Story Books Teachers' Guide Red Level Set B*, p.35.

- Cut out small pictures from a magazine: four red things, four blue things and four yellow things. Paste each picture onto the front of an envelope and write a small caption, e.g.

Arrange the children in a circle and randomly place the envelopes in the middle. Write the following instruction onto several cards, inserting different objects in the spaces:

> **Red and yellow and blue,**
> **This is what I want you to do.**
> **Find the one with ...(e.g. a red hat)**
> **And give it to a friend.**

Have the children chant this message with you. Select someone to begin the game. The child finds the correct envelope and gives it to another child. This child has the next turn. This is a particularly enjoyable game and can be altered easily, e.g. by changing the captions and pictures to numerals or high frequency words.

Books to share and compare
- **Colours Everywhere,**
  Tana Hoban,
  Greenwillow Books, 1995.
- **Let's Look at Colours,**
  Nicola Tuxworth,
  Lorenz Books, 1996.
- **Red,**
  Blue,
  Yellow,
  Gabrielle Woolfitt,
  Wayland, 1991.
- **Red Light, Green Light,**
  Margaret Wise Brown,
  Scholastic, 1992.
- **All About Colour,**
  Irene Yates,
  Belitha, 1997.
- **Brown Cow, Green Grass and**
  Mellow Yellow Sun,
  Ellen Jackson,
  Hyperion Books, 1995.
- **Flora and the Strawberry Red**
  Birthday Party,
  Ronda and David Armitage,
  Viking, 1997.

Curriculum

**Mathematics —
Geometry (Space and Location)**

The children will:
- explore positional relationships
- respond to directions
- describe the position of objects

**Blackline masters 7 and 8,
pp.27–28.**

Look Up, Look Down

Look Up, Look Down uses a children's game, 'Teddy Bear Hunt', to reinforce the spatial concepts of 'up' and 'down'. The text offers opportunities for prediction and confirmation. Further positional vocabulary, i.e. 'out' and 'into', can be reinforced after reading the book.

Creating the atmosphere

- Read *Ben's treasure hunt* (PM Story Books Red Level), and talk about the places where Ben looked for his treasure.

Focusing on the book — guided reading

- Read the title. Look at the cover photograph and point out that the girl is looking up as she reaches for the teddy bear. Look at the photograph on the title page and point out that the boy is looking down into the basket.
- p.2 — Clap to the rhythm of the words as the class reads them aloud together.
- pp.4–5 — Identify the teddy bear imprint on the clue card on p.5. Talk about why the swing will be in the garden. Discuss the positional vocabulary of 'looking up on the swing'. Talk about the question 'Can you find a teddy bear?'.
- pp.6–11 — Note that the teddy bear imprint continues on each clue card. Discuss the information each clue provides, i.e. what to look for and where to go to look for it.
- pp.12–15 — Ask the children to read these pages to find out where the teddy bears are hidden.
- p.16 — Ask the children "How can you tell that all of the teddy bears have been found?"

Going beyond the book

- Show each child how to make a teddy bear finger puppet. Cut out a teddy bear shape from a piece of card and use sticky tape to attach a finger holding space at the back.

- Talk about places in the classroom where the children could hide their teddy bear finger puppets. Make photocopied clue cards. Show the children how to add information giving clues where to look. Each child can read another child's clue card and hunt to find the teddy bear.

PREPARED PHOTOCOPY.   COMPLETED COPY.

- As an alternative activity to the previous one, find places around the classroom using only 'up' or 'down' positions, e.g. up on the teacher's desk, up on the bench, down in Jason's shoe, down by a chair. The children could draw pictures showing where to put their teddy bears. Paste the pictures into a book for shared reading.

*Can you see
Jane's teddy
bear?*

*He is down in
Jane's shoe.*

- Get the children to take their teddy bear finger puppets to the school playground. As a problem solving activity have the children show what their teddy bears can do, e.g. take a teddy bear up the ladder and down the slide, make a teddy bear sit on a bar or go into a tunnel.

- When you return to the classroom, ask the children to make playgrounds for their teddy bear finger puppets. Give the children strips of card, pipecleaners, string, cylinders, scissors, glue, sticky tape, and a base board. When they finish their playgrounds, the children can explain what their puppets are able to do on them.

- Read and dramatise *Bears in the Night* (Stan and Jan Berenstain, Collins, 1971). Dramatise the story to reinforce positional vocabulary, e.g. out the window, down the tree, over the bridge. Make a class or group mural and write captions to show the events of the story in sequence. Extend this activity by making a set of cards the same as the captions for the children to match with the pictures.

- Explore the positional vocabulary of 'up' and 'down' further by talking about things that the children can do. List these things and use them to make a shared book, individual books or a concertina wall story.

- Discuss things that can go up, e.g. a kite can go up, a plane can go up, a bird can fly up into a tree, etc. Discuss things that go down. Make a flip chart about things that go up or down.

 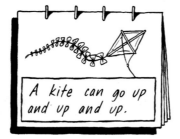

Books to share and compare
- **Look Up, Look Down**,
  Tana Hoban,
  Greenwillow Books, 1992.
- **What's Inside?**,
  Anthea Sieveking,
  Frances Lincoln, 1989.
- **Dog In, Cat Out**,
  Gillian Rubinstein and Ann James,
  Omnibus, 1997.
- **Bears in the Night**,
  Stan and Jan Berenstain,
  Collins, 1971.

Curriculum

Mathematics — Number

The children will:
- identify groups of two
- form sets of two and match using one-to-one correspondence
- recognise the invariance of a set of two

Blackline masters 9 and 10, pp.29–30.

Two Eyes, Two Ears

This book initiates purposeful counting as children recognise the relationship of the number 'two' with themselves, their families and their belongings.

Creating the atmosphere

- Bring a mirror into the classroom. Have the children look at themselves in the mirror and talk about what they can see one of, e.g. one nose, one mouth, one head, one body; and what they can see two of, e.g. two ears, two eyes, two arms, etc.
- Ask each child to sketch a self-portrait. Keep these self-portraits.

Focusing on the book — guided reading

- Read the title and discuss the cover and title page photographs. Identify the boy as the main character. Ask, "What does he have two of?"
- pp.2–3 — Ask the children what they can see two of in the photograph. Draw the children's suggestions and add labels.
- pp.4–5 — Have the children touch their own eyes, ears and lips. Discuss the way their mouths have two lips.
- pp.6–7 — Have the children show their own two hands and two arms.
- pp.8–9 — Ask a child to demonstrate how to put on a sweater. Talk about the actions involved. Talk about the two things a sweater has.
- pp.10–11 — Ask the children to point to their own legs and feet.
- pp.12–13 — Talk about the concept of 'a pair'. Discuss why we say a pair of socks and a pair of shoes. Find the two socks and the two shoes.
- pp.14–15 — Talk about why the brothers might look alike. Generate some reasons why, e.g. they are both the same age, they are both the same height, they are both wearing the same clothes.
- p.16 — Ensure that the children understand what is meant by 'twins', i.e. a closely related or associated pair. Have the children identify all the things in the photograph which are alike.

Going beyond the book

- Give the children back the self-portrait sketches they drew before reading the book. Ask the children to improve these sketches. Have the children put the sketches side by side and talk about why one is better than the other.
- Books, finger plays and number rhymes all help children to become familiar with number names. Share rhymes like 'One, two, buckle my shoe' or 'One, two, three, four, five, once I caught a fish alive'.
- Explore sets which have two objects.

Make sets of two, using objects which are the same,
    e.g. two counters, two cars, two blocks.

Make patterns with sets of two,
    e.g. two iceblock sticks in a repeated pattern.

Make repeated patterns of two,
    e.g. two blue beads, two red beads, two blue beads, two red beads.

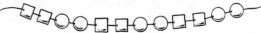

Two Eyes, Two Ears

- Talk about what having a partner means. Ask the children to find a partner. Discuss the things you do with a partner, e.g. carry messages, share morning news, play games, do folk dances. Each child could draw and write about something that he or she does with a partner.

Ask the children to find partners, and explore different ways of arranging themselves to make patterns of two, e.g. two standing up, two sitting down, two standing up, two sitting down. The children could draw pictures of these patterns to reinforce understandings.

- Discuss actions that the children can do with their hands. Mime the different actions and make a concertina booklet about them.

- The concept of 'two' could be reinforced by the children choosing between two items. Select two items, e.g. orange juice and lemonade. Ask the children to imagine they are on a picnic and they can choose only one drink. Have the children make small self-portraits. Make a two-column chart. Ask the children to paste their self-portraits onto the column of their choice.

- Make a high-frequency word lotto game. As the child recognises each word, he or she puts the correct card onto the space on the word lotto sheet, i.e. the two words are the same. Alternatively, pairs of high frequency words can be written onto flash cards and used to play 'Memory' or 'Concentration'.

come		went
	my	
to		here

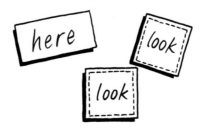

Books to share and compare
- ***Willy Can Count***,
  Anne Rockwell,
  Arcade Publishing, 1989.
- ***Look and Learn Counting***,
  George Siede and Donna Preis,
  Evans Brothers, 1994.
- ***Triplets***,
  Felix Pirani,
  ABC, London, 1990.

Curriculum

Mathematics — Geometry

The children will:
- recognise that everything has shape
- name some shapes
- recognise that shapes help them to identify what things are

Blackline masters 11 and 12, pp.31–32.

A Roof and a Door

A Roof and a Door provides meaningful opportunities for children to observe, discuss, compare, discover and generalise about the properties of shape and space around them.

Creating the atmosphere

- Read *PM Alphabet Starters*. Talk about what shapes the children can see in the photograph of the house on p.3 of *A Roof and a Door*. Re-read *A house* (PM Starters One).

Focusing on the book — guided reading

- Read the title. Look at the cover photograph. Talk about the house and garden that the children are making. Name the shapes. Look at the door on the title page and discuss the shapes that are there.
- pp.2–3 — Explain that the girl is showing the boy her house. Look at the different shapes that are on the house.
- pp.4–5 — Discuss the shape of the roof line, the windows and the door. Encourage the children to discover additional shapes within each item.
- pp.6–7 — Ensure that the children understand that the girl is making her picture using the discoveries she has made about her family house.
- pp.8–9 — Discuss the shapes that the girl used to make her house and path. Encourage the children to name what part each shape represented.
- pp.10–11 — Encourage the children to predict the shapes that the boy may find in his garden.
- pp.12–13 — Talk about the tree shapes with the children, and point out that one is like a circle and the other is like a triangle. Compare these with tree shapes in the school grounds or neighbourhood. Talk about the shapes on the gate and letter box, and the fence that 'goes around the garden'.
- Ask the children whether the boy is using any shapes from his family garden in his picture.
- p.16 — Look for the red window that is like a square, the yellow sun that is like a circle, etc. Talk about the question mark, which asks the children to respond with an answer.

Going beyond the book

- The children could make their own shape pictures of houses and gardens. They could use coloured paper, cardboard, felt pieces or wooden shapes. Prepare the shapes by cutting them into sizes and proportions which fit easily together. The children can sort the shapes into containers for easy access and storage.

- Put some objects into a paper bag. Ask the children to put their hands into the paper bag and identify the shapes by touch alone.

A Roof and a Door

- Take the children for a 'shape walk' around the school. Classify the shapes on fences, gates, buildings, windows, concrete markings, playground equipment, trees and gardens. Encourage the children to discuss the shapes, e.g. "Look, this window is like a square." Take photographs during the walk. Use the photographs to make an enlarged book. Classify the shapes in the photographs and write captions.

- Provide boxes, blocks and containers so that the children can make models of robots, rockets, houses, cranes or towers. Have the children use their palms and fingers to feel the shape of each surface. Talk about the sides, corners and edges so that the children can feel and see them.

- Make a book about each shape. The children can draw pictures, and then cut and paste them.

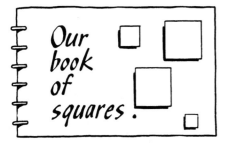 

- Take the children for a walk in the carpark. Look for shapes on cars. Encourage the children to qualify their responses, e.g. "The wheels are round like circles", or "This window is like a rectangle."

- Discuss photograph frame shapes. The children can draw photos of themselves and cut them into shapes to make a photomontage.

- Play the game of 'I spy', adapting it to identify objects in the classroom by their shapes, e.g. "I spy with my little eye something that is like a circle. What might it be?" When the children understand how the game is played, it could become an independent small group or paired activity.

- Give the children water and large paint brushes so they can draw shapes on the concrete.

- Sing and dance to 'Round and round the village' in *On with the Dance* (PM Readalongs: On with the Dance).

Books to share and compare

- **Shapes**,
  George Siede and Donna Preis,
  Evans Brothers, 1993.
- **Ready-Steady-Go Shapes**,
  Jane Salt,
  Kingfisher, 1990.
- **About Shapes**,
  Richard Allington,
  Raintree Publications, 1979.
- **Squares and Cubes**,
  Sally Morgan,
  Wayland, 1994.
- **Spot's Big Book of Colours, Shapes and Numbers**,
  Eric Hill,
  Puffin, 1994.

Children deepen their understanding through a kinaesthetic learning approach.

Using the Blackline masters

Before using each Blackline master, prepare the children using the following suggestions.

Blackline master 1   *Tall Things*
- Talk about the things in the book which are tall.
- Read p.16 again and discuss the concept of seriation.
- Read each sentence on the Blackline master together.
- Discuss how each picture will be taller than the one before.

Blackline master 2   *Tall Things*
- Have the children mark how tall they are on a wall chart.
- Explain to the children how to draw themselves as tall as the height on the Blackline master.
- Read each sentence on the Blackline master together.
- Discuss how to draw someone who is not as tall.

Blackline master 3   *Eggs for Breakfast*
- Recall the concept of one egg for one egg cup in the non-fiction book.
- Read the Blackline master instructions together.

Blackline master 4   *Eggs for Breakfast*
- Read the numerals and number names.
- Count each set of objects. Demonstrate how to write the number name that tells 'how many' to complete the sentences.
- Explain to the children how to draw a set of objects in each box.

Blackline master 5   *Red and Blue and Yellow*
- Talk about the examples of red, blue and yellow in *Red and Blue and Yellow*.
- Read the captions on the Blackline master with the children. Encourage them to use the picture clues.
- Ask the children to suggest things that can be blue.

Blackline master 6   *Red and Blue and Yellow*
- Have the children colour each centre rectangle with the correct colour.
- Re-read the book. Talk about items which are red and blue and yellow.
- Encourage the children to name other items which are these colours.
- Have the children share their responses with the rest of the group.

Blackline master 7   *Look Up, Look Down*
- Read the book to recall the teddy bear clues.
- Read the words in the boxes on the Blackline master.
- Read the sentences on the Blackline master with the children and discuss what the missing word in each sentence will be.
- Ask the children to complete the sentences and draw the teddy bear for each picture.

Blackline master 8   *Look Up, Look Down*
- Take the children outside. Discuss what they can see when they look up. Discuss what they can see when they look down.
- On returning to the classroom, read the sentences on the Blackline master and look at the pictures.
- When finished, ask the children to read their responses.

Blackline master 9   *Two Eyes, Two Ears*
- Discuss how the children will draw themselves.
- Show the children how to put a ✓ or a ✗ in the boxes to assess their drawings.
- Read the sentences and say the missing words.
- Tell the children how many of each object to draw.

Blackline master 10   *Two Eyes, Two Ears*
- Give each child a piece of grey paper which will be used for their completed teddy bear.
- Read each sentence and encourage the children to explain the instruction in their own words.
- Demonstrate how to cut and paste, beginning with the body and head.
- Ask the children to draw additional features to complete the teddy bear.

Blackline master 11   *A Roof and a Door*
- Read the sentence on the Blackline master together.
- Ask the children about the shapes they will use to draw a house, a fence and a gate. Encourage them to refer to *A Roof and a Door*.
- When the children have finished their pictures, help them to assess the details. Let them put the ✓ or ✗ in the boxes.

Blackline master 12   *A Roof and a Door*
- Read the instructions. Ask the children to colour the small shapes in the sentences.
- Encourage the children to look closely at the shape prompts before they identify the corresponding ones in the large picture.
- Ask the children to explain the instructions in their own words before they proceed.

My name is _____

I am tall.

Mum is tall.

A giraffe is tall.

A crane is very tall.

My name is _____

I am tall
like this.

_____ is tall
like me.

_____ is tall
like me, too.

_____ is **not**
tall like me.

_____ comes
up to here.

Tall Things © Nelson ITP, 1998.

My name is _____

Put an ⬭ in each 🥚.

Put a 🐟 in each 🥣.

Put a 🕯 on each 🧁.

Put a 🌼 in each 🪴.

My name is _____

1	2	3	4
one	two	three	four

Here are _____ egg cups.

Here are _____ eggs.

Here are _____ plates.

Here are _____ spoons.

Here is _____ mat.

1	2	3	4
one	two	three	four

My name is _____

| red | yellow |

A chick can be _____.

Corn can be _____.

A strawberry can be _____.

Cherries can be _____.

A banana can be _____.

The sun looks _____.

What can be blue?

My name is _____

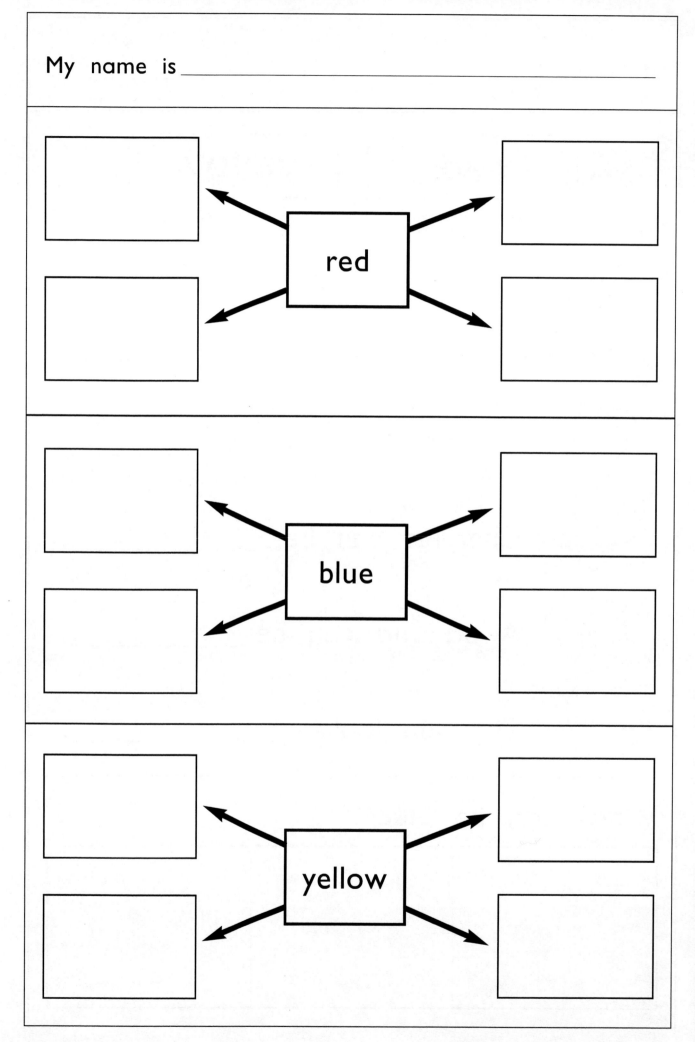

red

blue

yellow

My name is _____

| up | down |

The teddy bear

is _____ in the toy box.

The teddy bear

is _____ on the chair.

The teddy bear

is _____ in the basket.

The teddy bear

is _____ on the swing.

My name is _____

I look **up**.

I can see...

I look **down**.

I can see...

| a roof | a cloud | a tree | a bird | a chimney |

| shoes | grass | a path | flowers | leaves |

My name is _____

This is me.
yes   no
✓ or ✗

I have two eyes. 👁 👁 ☐

I have two ears. 👂 👂 ☐

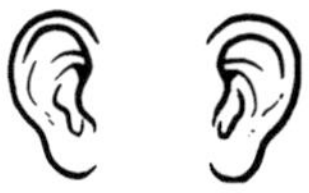

I have two lips. 👄 ☐

| two |

Here are my _____ arms.

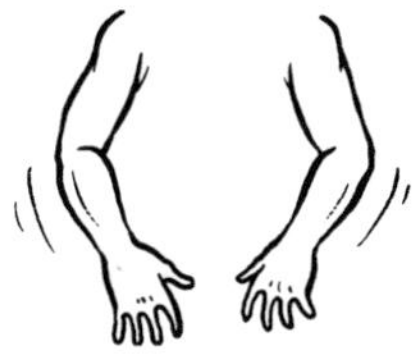

Here are my _____ legs.

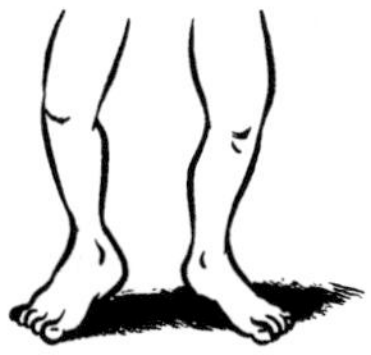

Here are my _____ socks.

Here are my _____ shoes.

Draw 2  ☂	Draw 2  🐱	Draw two  🌳	Draw two  🌸

My name is _____

Cut ✂ and paste 🫙

1. Here are 2 arms
   for my teddy bear.

2. Here are 2 legs
   for my teddy bear.

3. Here are 2 ears
   for my teddy bear.

My name is _____

Here is a house with a fence and a gate.

My picture has a ○.
My picture has a □.

My picture has a □.
My picture has a △.

My name is _____

1. Colour the big △ red.
   Colour the little △ green.

2. Colour the big ▭ blue.
   Colour the little ▯ 's yellow.

3. Colour the big ☐ blue.
   Colour the little ☐'s yellow.

4. Colour the big ◯ green.
   Colour the little ◯'s red.

A Roof and a Door © Nelson ITP, 1998.
This page may be photocopied for educational use within the purchasing institution.